*I love that you're my*

# Boyfriend

*because*

I Love You Because Books
www.riverbreezepress.com

# To My Boyfriend

Love, _____

Date: _____

# The best thing about you is your

_____

# Thank you for being patient with me when

_____

You have wonderful

_____

# I remember when we

_____

# You make me feel special when

_____

You have brought
more

_____

into my life

*I love when you tell me about*

_____

*I love when we*

_____

*together*

*You taught me how to*

_____

*I know you love me because*

# I wish I could

---

## as well as
## you do

*I love that we have the same*

_____

# I am amazed at your ability to

_____

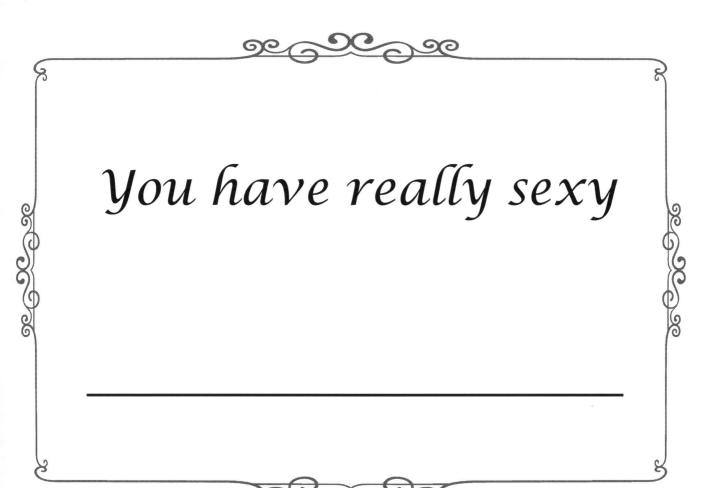

You have really sexy

_____

# You make me laugh when you

_____

*I wish I had more time to*

_____

*with you*

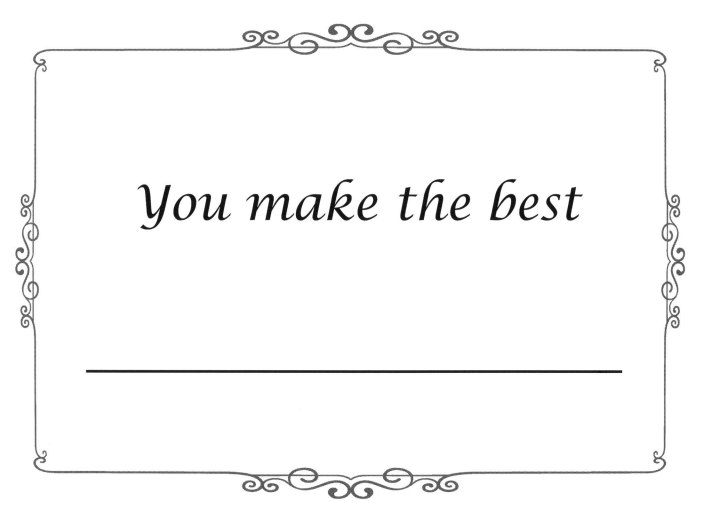

You make the best

_____

# You have inspired me to

_____

*If I could give
you anything it
would be*

_____

*I would love to go*

_____

*with you*

You are
there for me when

_____

*I love you
because you are*

_____

Made in the USA
Columbia, SC
19 December 2019